Phèdre

PHÈDRE

DOVER THRIFT EDITIONS

Jean Racine

Translated by
Wallace Fowlie

DOVER PUBLICATIONS, INC.
MINEOLA, NEW YORK

DOVER THRIFT EDITIONS

General Editor: Paul Negri

Theatrical Rights

Bibliographical Note

This Dover edition, first published in 2017, contains the unabridged text of *Phaedra*, as printed in the volume *Classical French Drama*, published as part of the Library of World Drama Series by Bantam Books, Inc., in 1962 and reprinted by Dover in its entirety in 1997.

Library of Congress Cataloging-in-Publication Data

Names: Racine, Jean, 1639–1699, author ; translated by Wallace Fowlie. | Fowlie, Wallace, 1908–1998, translator.
Title: Phedre / Jean Racine.
Other titles: Pháedre. English
Description: Mineola, New York : Dover Publications, 2017. | Series: Dover thrift editions
Identifiers: LCCN 2017027320 | ISBN 9780486817132 (paperback) | ISBN 048681713X (paperback)
Subjects: LCSH: Phaedra (Greek mythology—Drama. | BISAC: DRAMA / General.
Classification: LCC PQ1898 .A336 2017 | DDC 842/.4—dc23
LC record available at https://lccn.loc.gov/2017027320

Manufactured in the United States by LSC Communications
81713X01   2017
www.doverpublications.com

Note

JEAN RACINE (1639–1699) was educated at Jansenist schools, especially at Port-Royal, where he lived between the ages of fifteen and eighteen. The Jansenists stressed, in addition to the Bible and theology, the study of Greek. They were Catholic priests, followers of Jansenius, who emphasized, in their moral teaching, a severe concept of man's sinful nature. Jansenism, which undoubtedly explains some of Racine's psychology, has come to designate a belief in the fundamental corruption of human nature, or at least in its weakness, its impotency. The picture it gives of man as victim of his instincts and passions is in accord with the characterizations of many of Racine's heroines.

As a young playwright in Paris, where he met Boileau and Molière, Racine broke with Port-Royal. His first success was *Andromaque*, in 1667. *Phèdre* was written and produced ten years later, in 1677, and by then his enemies formed such a strong opposition to the play that Racine left the theater and became reconciled with his former teachers at Port-Royal. For Madame de Maintenon's school at Saint-Cyr, he wrote two Biblical plays, *Esther* and *Athalie*.

The achievement of Racine as dramatist is due in part to his theory of tragic action and to his penetration as psychologist, but it is also in part due to his poetic gifts, to the elegance of his expression, to the beauty of his style. Racine's particular triumph is in the fusion he performed between meaning and music, between tragic sentiment and the pure sound of his alexandrine line. He was familiar with the style of the *précieux*, and there are elements of preciosity throughout his tragedies. But on the whole he rejected superfluous ornaments and excluded unusual words from his vocabulary. When the occasion called for it, Racine could write lines as vibrantly eloquent as those of Corneille. French poetry was not to know again such human poignancy and such stylistic simplicity and dramatic meaning as Racine, at his best, represented until the publication of Baudelaire's poetry in the nineteenth century.

Racine did not bring any new formulas to the art of tragedy. The unities presented no difficulties for him. This is made clear in his various *préfaces*. If Corneille solved the conflict between will and passion by the triumph of will, Racine solved it in the triumph of passion. The leading characters in Corneille are men, whereas the leading characters in Racine are women. *Phèdre*, like all of his tragedies, begins when the dramatic action is well advanced, when the end is not far off. The action takes place on an inner level. If a violent act—such as the appearance of the sea monster and the death of Hippolytus in *Phèdre*—does take place, it is not shown, but narrated.

Phèdre is the great example in the theater of Racine of a woman driven by passion and all the conflicting emotions of modesty, hope, shame, remorse, jealousy, repentance. In the psychological sense, the role is the richest in the entire classical repertory. Phèdre passes through four or five momentous phases of suffering. At first, she hides her passion and wishes to die. When she believes Theseus is dead, she acknowledges her passion. On his return, she allows the greater crime of calumny to be committed. Repentant at the end, she makes a public confession and takes her life.

Based principally on the tragedy of Euripides, Racine's *Phèdre* has preserved the atmosphere of terrifying and supernatural legends without ever sacrificing the universal human truth of the story. The passion of Phèdre is so intense and so thwarted that she becomes the persecutor and the enemy of the man she loves. Love and hate are, in the dramaturgy of Racine, strong sentiments which are difficult to dissociate or separate. The idealistic chivalric love which dominates the plays of Corneille is replaced in Racine by a possessive and brutal type of love. Racinian love is the negation of the freedom which can be seen in the psychology of Corneille's heroes and heroines.

Racine constantly doubts the power of man's reason and intelligence to aid in the solution of a moral or psychological dilemma. Here he recalls a Jansenistic suspicion that the heart of man is easily duped by itself. *Les Maximes* of La Rochefoucauld testified at the same time in the seventeenth century to man's fundamental dishonesty with himself. The Greek sense of faith which was often a force exterior to the protagonist is transposed by Racine to an inner passion, to a personal malady which incites remorse and scorn of self. Phèdre speaks of her guilt being so strong that she tries to escape from daylight.

If Racine emphasizes the subject of love in his tragedies, it is because love is the blindest of all passions, the one most deliberately pointed toward self-destruction. Such a theme as ambition, for example, would have to by definition maintain a greater lucidity and self-esteem. The whole meaning of tragedy is revived and explored by Racine in his treatment of love.

The tragic is irremediable for this poet. Catastrophe is omnipresent from the very beginning of the play. It is a necessity for Phèdre. It is a part of her very nature. In every century the literary art of tragedy is the picture of man confronting a superior force which defeats him. In this sense, Le Cid is not a tragedy, but Phèdre is. Even for the Greeks, fate is not in the power of the gods; it is beyond them. It is a force that cannot be named. It is not identical with the scientific determinism of the nineteenth century, nor is it exactly comparable to the Jansenist predestination of the seventeenth century. It seems to be in Racine, and especially in Phèdre, an inner psychological determinism, a state of the heart in which the drama unfolds. In its implacable aspect it resembles the rigors of Jansenist theology. The protagonist of Racine is a victim to whom no choice is offered. Phèdre can find no way out of the labyrinth of her passion. And yet there are two possible explanations of the catastrophe in Phèdre: a human explanation in terms of passion, and a divine explanation in terms of Venus and Neptune.

Characters

THESEUS, *son of Aegeus, King of Athens*
PHÈDRE, *wife of Theseus, daughter of Minos and Pasiphaë*
HIPPOLYTUS, *son of Theseus and Antiope, Queen of the Amazons*
ARICIA, *princess of the royal blood of Athens*
THERAMENES, *tutor of Hippolytus*
OENONE, *nurse and confidante of Phèdre*
ISMENE, *confidante of Aricia*
PANOPE, *lady-in-waiting to Phèdre*
GUARDS

SCENE: *Troezen, a city of the Peloponnesus.*

Phèdre

ACT I

Scene 1. *Hippolytus, Theramenes.*

HIPPOLYTUS.   I have made up my mind, Theramenes.
  I am leaving this place; I am leaving beautiful Troezen.
  My idleness shames me
  because of the deadly doubt filling my heart.
  Separated from my father for more than six months,
  I know nothing of his fate.
  I do not even know the place where he hides.
THERAMENES.   My lord, where will you go to look for him?
  To placate your justified fear,
  I have already crossed the two seas Corinth separates.   10
  I have asked about Theseus of the people on those shores
  where the Acheron disappears into Hades.
  I have visited Elis, and leaving Taenarus behind me,
  I went as far as the sea into which Icarus fell.
  With what new hope and in what happy land
  do you expect to discover the trace of his passing?
  And who can tell whether the King your father
  wants the mystery of his absence to be known?
  and whether, when with you we fear for his life,
  that hero, at peace and concealing a new love,   20
  is not waiting until his deceived mistress . . .
HIPPOLYTUS.   Stop, Theramenes, and show respect for Theseus.
  He has left all his youthful errors behind him
  and is not detained now by any unworthy obstacle.
  By her prayers Phèdre changed his fatal inconstancy
  and for a long time has feared no rival.
  I will be doing my duty if I look for him,

N.B. An index of proper names follows the translation.

1

and I shall get away from Troezen which I no longer want to
  see.

THERAMENES.   My lord, for how long have you feared the
    presence

of this peaceful town you loved as a boy,   30
and which I have seen you prefer
to the noise and pomp of Athens and the court?
What danger, or rather, what sorrow, sends you away?

HIPPOLYTUS.   The time of happiness is over. Everything has
    changed

since the gods sent to these shores
the daughter of Minos and Pasiphaë.

THERAMENES.   I understand. I know the cause of your suffering.
Phèdre makes you suffer and humiliates you.
She is a hostile stepmother who, when she saw you,
tried to send you into exile.   40
But her hatred, once fixed on you,
has disappeared or has diminished.
And what dangers can this dying woman,
who wants to die, make you endure?
Phèdre, struck down by a sickness she will not name,
tired of herself and the daylight around her,
cannot construct any plots against you.

HIPPOLYTUS.   Her vain enmity is not what I fear.
Hippolytus is fleeing another enemy.
Let me confess it. I am fleeing Aricia,   50
the last fatal descendant of a house conspiring against us.

THERAMENES.   Are you, also, my lord, persecuting her?
Never did the gentle sister of the Pallantides
participate in the plots of her treacherous brothers!
How can you hate her innocent charms?

HIPPOLYTUS.   If I hated her, I would not flee her.

THERAMENES.   My lord, may I try to explain your flight?
Is it possible you have ceased being proud Hippolytus,
the implacable enemy of the laws of love
and of the yoke which Theseus wore so often?   60
Does Venus, whom your pride scorned for so long a time,
want at last to justify Theseus?
And placing you in company with other mortals,
has she forced you to light incense on her altars?
Are you in love, my lord?

HIPPOLYTUS.   You are bold to ask this question.
You who have known my heart since the beginning of my life,

can you ask me to disavow shamefully
the sentiments of so proud and scornful a heart?
My pride which amazes you was fed me   70
with my mother's milk and her Amazon pride.
When I reached an older age
I approved of all I learned about myself.
Serving me then with sincere zeal,
you told me the story of my father.
You know how my soul, attentive to your voice,
gloried in the tales of his noble exploits
when you portrayed him as an intrepid hero
consoling men for the absence of Hercules,
killing monsters and pursuing brigands: 80
Procrustus, Cercyon, Sirron, and Sinnis,
and scattering the bones of the giant of Epidaurus,
and saving Crete with the blood of the Minotaur.
But when you told me the less glorious deeds,
his promise of marriage offered in a hundred places—
Helen stolen from her parents in Sparta,
Salamis comforting the tears of Periboea,
and others whose names he has forgotten,
overconfident hearts whom his passion deceived,
Ariadne telling her story of injustice to the rocks,   90
Phèdre, brought to Athens for a legitimate cause—
as I listened embarrassed to those stories,
you remember how I urged you to shorten them,
happy if I could efface from memory
the unworthy half of so noble a life!
Can it be that now I, in my turn, am bound?
Can it be that now the gods have humiliated me?
I am more to be scorned in my cowardly sighs
because so many honors were the excuse for Theseus.
I have destroyed no monsters   100
and have therefore no right to weaken as he did.
Even if my pride could be softened,
should I have chosen Aricia for my conqueror?
Can't my bewildered senses remember any longer
the eternal obstacle which separates us?
My father disapproves of her, and a severe decree
forbids that her brothers should ever have nephews.
He fears an offspring from such a guilty line,
and wishes to bury their name with their sister.
He claims she is under his control until death,   110

and never will the marriage fire be lighted.
Can I espouse her rights against an angry father?
Shall I be the example of a presumptuous action,
and in this mad love, will my youth . . .

THERAMENES.　My lord, once your fate is inscribed,
Heaven can take no account of your reasonings.
Theseus opened your eyes in wishing to close them,
and his hate, exciting a rebellious passion,
gives to his enemy a new grace.
But why be afraid of a chaste love?　　　　　　　　　120
If it is sweet to you, why not taste it?
Will you always be restrained by scruples?
Do you fear losing your way in following Hercules?
Think of the strong wills which Venus has overcome.
Where would you be, you who fight Venus,
If Antiope, opposing her laws,
had not desired Theseus with modest ardor?
Why pretend with these proud words?
Confess it and all will change. For several days now
you have seemed a proud and solitary figure, rarely　　130
driving a chariot along the shore,
or, learned in that art invented by Neptune,
bending to a halter an untamed horse.
The forests resound less often now with our cries.
Your eyes have grown heavy with some inner torment.
There is no more doubt of it. You are in love and you are
　　suffering.
You are perishing from a malady you conceal.
Has beautiful Aricia cast a spell over you?

HIPPOLYTUS.　I am leaving, Theramenes, to search for my father.
THERAMENES.　Will you not see Phèdre before going, my lord?　140
HIPPOLYTUS.　It is my intention. You may inform her.
I will see her, for my duty demands this.

　　　　　　　　　　　　　　　　　　　　　　[OENONE *enters.*]

What new woe has upset her faithful Oenone?

Scene 2. *Hippolytus, Oenone, Theramenes.*

OENONE.　Alas, my lord, what sorrow is equal to mine?
The Queen is approaching the end of her fate.
In vain I have been keeping watch over her day and night.
In my arms she is dying from a malady she hides from me.
An endless disorder reigns in her mind.

The suffering of her mind allows her no rest.
She wants to see the daylight, and her deep grief
insists that I send everyone away.
She is coming. . . .

HIPPOLYTUS.   I understand. I will leave her alone.   10
My presence would be displeasing to her.

Scene 3. *Phèdre, Oenone.*

PHÈDRE.   Let us go no farther. Stay here, Oenone.
I cannot stand up. My strength has gone.
My eyes are dazzled by the daylight I see
and my trembling knees are giving way.
Alas! [*She sits down.*]

OENONE.   Would that our tears might appease the gods!

PHÈDRE.   These useless ornaments and these veils are heavy on
    me.
Some irksome hand, by weaving these knots,
has tied my hair tight over my head.
Everything pains and harms me, and conspires to harm me.   10

OENONE.   Your wishes are destroyed as soon as they are
    expressed!
You yourself, condemning your unjust plans,
urged us just now to dress and prepare you.
You yourself, remembering your earlier strength,
wanted to appear and behold again the light of day.
But as soon as you see it, you turn to hide
as if you hate the very light you came to see.

PHÈDRE.   O Sun, noble and shining author of a wretched
    family,
whose daughter my mother boasted of being,
and who perhaps now blushes at seeing my shame,   20
I am here to see you for the last time.

OENONE.   Will you never renounce this cruel desire?
Am I to see you renouncing life
and making the funereal preparation of your death?

PHÈDRE.   Why am I not sitting in the shadow of the forests?
When shall I follow with my eyes
through the dust of the roads, a chariot racing along the
    course?

OENONE.   What did you say?

PHÈDRE.   I am a fool. Where am I and what
    did I say?

To what extremes did my desires and my mind wander?   30
I have lost my mind. The gods have deprived me of it.
Oenone, shame is written over my face.
You can see too clearly my shameful grief,
and my eyes, in spite of myself, are filling with tears.
OENONE.   If you must blush, let it be from that silence
which still embitters the violence of your woe.
Rebellious to our attention and deaf to our speech,
will you without feeling let your days end?
What madness limits them in the midst of their course?
What witchcraft or what poison has dried up their source?   40
Three times have shadows darkened the sky
since sleep entered your eyes.
And three times has day dispelled the blackness of night
since your body has languished without food.
By what terrifying plan are you being tempted?
What right have you to attack your own life?
You offend the gods who are authors of that life.
You fail your husband to whom you are joined in pledge.
And finally you fail your wretched children
whom you place under a rigorous yoke.   50
Remember that a single day will take their mother away
and give hope to the son of the foreign woman,
to that implacable enemy of your family,
the son who was carried in the womb of an Amazon,
Hippolytus. . . .
PHÈDRE.   Stop!
OENONE.   My reproach moves you!
PHÈDRE.   Wretched woman, what name did you utter?
OENONE.   How justified is your anger!
I am glad to see you startled by that fatal name.   60
You must live and not allow a Scythian's son,
as he crushes your children under his hateful authority,
to command the noblest offspring of Greece and of the gods.
Do not delay. Each moment may be mortal.
Bring back now some of your impaired strength
while your life, on the point of being extinguished,
may still endure in its flame and be rekindled.
PHÈDRE.   I have too far prolonged its guilty length.
OENONE.   What kind of remorse torments you?
What crime has brought about such bewilderment?   70
Have your hands been soiled by innocent blood?
PHÈDRE.   Thanks to heaven my hands are not criminal.

Would that my heart were as innocent as they are!
OENONE.　What terrible project have you conceived
　that your heart is so anguished by it?
PHÈDRE.　I have said enough to you. Spare me the rest.
　I wish to die in order not to make so cruel a confession.
OENONE.　Die and maintain your inhuman silence.
　But look for someone else to close your eyes.
　Although you are left with so little inner light,　　　80
　my soul will descend to the dead first.
　Many easy ways lead there,
　and my grief will choose the shortest.
　Cruel mistress, when did my devotion ever betray you?
　Remember that when you were born, my arms received you.
　I left everything for you, my country and my children.
　Is this the reward for my faithfulness?
PHÈDRE.　What can you hope for by thus forcing me?
　If I break my silence, horror will seize you.
OENONE.　What could you say that would be worse　　　90
　than the horror of seeing you die before my eyes?
PHÈDRE.　When you learn of my crime and the fate crushing me,
　I shall not die any less, and I shall die more guilty.
OENONE.　For the sake of the tears I have shed for you,
　here, at your faltering legs which I embrace,
　free my mind from this fatal doubt.
PHÈDRE.　Since you must know it, stand up.
OENONE.　　　　　　　　　　Speak! I am listening.
PHÈDRE.　What can I tell her? Where can I begin?
OENONE.　Stop offending me by this vain terror.　　　100
PHÈDRE.　The hatred of Venus and her fatal anger
　caused a perverted love to grow in my mother.
OENONE.　You must forget that. Hide that memory
　in unbroken silence throughout all the future.
PHÈDRE.　My sister Ariadne, wounded by a strange love,
　died at the rock where she was left.
OENONE.　Why are you saying this? What mortal torment
　urges you today to speak against all your family?
PHÈDRE.　It is the will of Venus that of all my family
　I shall die the last and the most wretched.　　　110
OENONE.　Are you in love?
PHÈDRE.　　　　　　　　I feel all the furies of love.
OENONE.　For whom?
PHÈDRE.　　　　　　　You are going to hear the extreme of all
　horrors.

I love . . . At his fatal name I shudder and tremble.
I love . . .
OENONE.   What man?
PHÈDRE.   You know the son of the Amazon woman,
the prince I persecuted for so long?
OENONE.   Hippolytus? All gods of heaven!   120
PHÈDRE.   It was you who named him.
OENONE.   My blood is congealed in all my veins.
The despair of this crime! The accursed race!
The unhappy voyage! Why did you have to come
to the shore of this dangerous land?
PHÈDRE.   My suffering comes from farther back. Scarcely was
    I bound
by the marriage law to the son of Aegeus,
my peace of mind and happiness seeming secure,
than Athens showed my proud enemy.
When I saw him I blushed and turned pale.   130
I grew troubled and anguished.
I was unable to see and unable to speak.
My body was either cold or on fire.
I recognized Venus and her fearful passion,
and the fatal torment of a family she persecutes.
I believed I could turn this aside by faithful prayers.
I built a temple in her name and adorned it.
Every hour I offered victims
and sought in their pierced flanks to recover my mind.
It was a powerless remedy for an incurable love.   140
Vainly I burned incense on the altars.
While my lips implored the name of the goddess,
I was worshipping Hippolytus. And seeing him constantly,
even at the foot of the altars where I made sacrifices,
I offered up everything to him I dared not name.
Wherever I went, I avoided him,
but I would see him in the features of his father.
At last I revolted against myself.
I stirred up my anger in order to persecute him.
In order to banish the enemy I idolized,   150
I pretended to show the meanness of an unjust stepmother.
I urged his exile and my endless cries
wrenched him away from the arms of his father.
Then I breathed, Oenone, and after his absence,
my days were less troubled and passed innocently.
Submissive to my husband, and hiding my torment,

I took care of the children of his unhappy marriage.
My fate made all this useless.
When Theseus himself brought me to Troezen,
I came upon the enemy I had sent away.   160
And the wound of love opened again.
It is no longer fire hidden in my veins.
It is Venus beating down on her prey with all her strength.
My crime now justly terrifies me.
I despise my life and my horrible love.
By dying I wanted to protect my honor,
and blot out from the day so black a flame.
I was unable to bear your tears and your questions.
So I have told you all, and I have no regret for this,
provided you will respect my death   170
and will not afflict me with unjust reproaches.
Do not try to recall
the remnants of a life which is ready to die.

Scene 4. *Phèdre, Oenone, Panope*.

PANOPE.   I tried to conceal the sad news from you,
     but I am forced to disclose it now.
     Death has taken your invincible husband.
     Only you are ignorant of this disaster.
PHÈDRE.   Panope, what are you saying?
PANOPE.   I say you are deceived,
     and there is no point in asking heaven for Theseus' return.
     From vessels now in the harbor,
     Hippolytus, his son, has just learned of his death.
     Athens is divided over the choice of a master.   10
     Some give their vote to your son the prince,
     and others, forgetful of the laws of the state,
     dare give their votes to the son of the foreign woman.
     It is even rumored that a bold plot
     plans to place on the throne Aricia and the blood of the
        Pallantides.
     I had to warn you of this peril.
     Even Hippolytus is making plans to leave for Athens,
     and it is feared that if he appears in this unforeseen turmoil,
     the fickle part of the populace will rally around him.
OENONE.   That's enough, Panope. The Queen has heard you   20
     and will not neglect this important warning.

Scene 5. *Phèdre, Oenone.*

OENONE.   My lady, I had given up urging you to live,
and already I had planned to follow you to the tomb.
I had no more desire to turn you away from it.
But this unexpected catastrophe forces other obligations on
    you.
Your position has changed and taken on a new meaning.
The King is dead, my lady, and you must take his place.
His death leaves you a son to whom you owe everything.
If you die, he will be a slave; if you live, he will be a king.
Who will be a support for him in this affliction?
There will be no one to dry his tears,   10
and his innocent cries, heard on high by the gods,
will work hardship on his mother and anger her ancestors.
You must live. You have nothing with which to reproach
    yourself.
Your love has become an ordinary love.
In his death Theseus has dissolved the complications
which made of your passion a fearful crime.
Hippolytus is less to be feared by you now.
You can see him without feeling guilty.
If he is convinced of your hate,
he may lead the revolt against you!   20
You must remove the error and bend his heart.
He is the king of this happy land. Troezen is his lot.
But he knows that the law gives to your son
the proud ramparts which Minerva has built.
Both of you have a natural enemy.
You should unite in order to oppose Aricia.
PHÈDRE.   I agree and I yield to your advice.
I will live, if I can move back into life,
and if the love for my son at this moment of mourning,
can bring life to my weak spirit.   30

ACT II

Scene 1. *Aricia, Ismene.*

ARICIA.   You say Hippolytus wants to see me here?
　He is looking for me and wants to make his farewell?
　Do you speak truthfully, Ismene? Or are you mistaken?
ISMENE.   This is the first reaction to the death of Theseus.
　You must be ready, my lady, to see from all sides
　people flocking to you who were rejected by Theseus.
　You are now the mistress of your fate
　and you may soon see all of Greece at your feet.
ARICIA.   Are you sure, Ismene, it is not an ill-founded rumor?
　Am I through being a slave? Have I no more enemies?   10
ISMENE.   No, my lady, the gods no longer oppose you.
　Theseus has joined the shades of your brothers.
ARICIA.   Is it known what accident ended his life?
ISMENE.   Unbelievable stories are circulating about his death.
　It is said he was the ravisher of a new mistress
　and was drowned in the sea because of his infidelity.
　It was even said—and this circulated widely—
　that he descended into hell with Pirithous
　where he saw the Cocytus and its dark banks,
　and appeared as a living man before the spirits of the dead;   20
　but that he could not get out from that wretched place
　and cross back over those shores which are never crossed twice.
ARICIA.   Am I to believe that a mortal, before his last hour,
　can penetrate the deep dwelling of the dead?
　What magic drew him to those fearful shores?
ISMENE.   Theseus is dead, my lady, and you alone doubt this.
　Athens is afraid. Troezen has learned of it
　and has already recognized Hippolytus as its king.
　Phèdre, in his palace, is trembling for her son

11

and asking advice of her worried friends.   30

ARICIA.   Do you believe that Hippolytus, more humane toward
  me
  than his father was, will lighten my slavery?
  Do you think he will pity my affliction?

ISMENE.   I do, my lady!

ARICIA.   But do you know the coldness of Hippolytus?
  What meager hope makes you think he will pity me
  and respect in me alone a sex he scorns?
  For some time he has been avoiding us
  and seeking places where we are not.

ISMENE.   I know what is said about his lack of feeling,   40
  but I have seen this proud Hippolytus in your presence,
  and as I watched him, the reports about his inhumanity
  increased my curiosity.
  His appearance did not correspond to these rumors.
  As soon as you looked at him, he seemed upset.
  His eyes, trying in vain to avoid looking,
  full of yearning, could not leave you.
  The name of lover offends his pride perhaps,
  but he has the eyes of a lover, if he has not the language.

ARICIA.   Dear Ismene, my heart listens avidly   50
  to your words which doubtless have no basis.
  You who know me, is it believable
  that the sad plaything of a pitiless fate,
  a heart like mine, fed on bitterness and tears,
  could know love and its mad grief?
  Descendant of a king and a noble family,
  I alone escaped the fury of the war.
  I lost, in the flower of their youth,
  six brothers. . . . They were the hope of a famous lineage!
  The sword cut them down, and the wet earth   60
  sorrowfully drank the blood of Erechtheus' nephews.
  Since their death, you know of the severe law
  which forbids the Greeks to pity me.
  It is feared that the rash flame of the sister
  will one day reanimate the ashes of her brothers.
  But you also know how scornfully
  I watched the worry of the suspicious conqueror.
  You know my long opposition to love
  and my gratitude to unjust Theseus
  whose rigorous law happily supported my scorn.   70
  My eyes at that time had not seen his son.

It is not that, shamefully bewitched by my eyes,
I love in him his beauty and his esteemed grace,
gifts by which nature has honored him,
which he himself repudiates or seems to ignore.
I love and esteem in him the noblest riches,
the virtues of his father, and not the weaknesses.
Let me confess it, I love the noble pride
which has never bent under the yoke of passion.
Vainly was Phèdre honored by the sighs of Theseus.   80
I am prouder than she, and I flee the easy glory
of winning an homage offered to a hundred others,
and entering a heart which has opened to so many.
What I want most and what excites me,
is to make an inflexible heart capitulate,
to convey suffering to an insensitive spirit,
to chain a captive stupefied by his irons,
vainly rebellious against a yoke he desires.
It was less difficult to disarm Hercules than Hippolytus.
He was conquered more often and defeated more quickly   90
and offered less glory to the one who tamed him.
But dear Ismene, see how imprudent I am!
All kinds of resistance will oppose me.
Humbly, in my anguish, you will perhaps hear me
lament over that same pride I admire today.
Might I have changed . . .

ISMENE.   You will hear this from Hippolytus himself.
He is coming here.

Scene 2. *Hippolytus, Aricia, Ismene.*

HIPPOLYTUS.   Before leaving,
I wanted to tell you what you may expect.
My father is dead. My legitimate fears
foretold the reasons of his prolonged absence.
Death alone, limiting my father's dazzling work,
was able to hide him from the universe.
At last the gods gave over to the murderous Fates
the friend, the companion, the successor of Hercules.
I suppose that your hate, refusing him his greatness,
hears with displeasure these names that are due him.   10
One hope softens my painful grief.
I am able to free you from a severe bondage.
I revoke the laws whose harshness I deplored.

You are free in body and heart.
Here in Troezen which is now my kingdom,
where once my ancestor Pittheus ruled,
and where immediately I was recognized as king,
I set you free. You are freer than I am.

ARICIA.   Your excessive kindness is embarrassing.
By honoring my misfortune with so generous an interest,   20
you place me, my lord, more than you realize,
under those austere laws from which you are freeing me.

HIPPOLYTUS.   Athens, uncertain over the choice of a successor,
speaks of you, names me, and does not forget the son of the
    Queen.

ARICIA.   They speak of me?

HIPPOLYTUS.   I am not deceived,
and know that an insolent law rejects me.
Greece reproaches me for my foreign mother.
But if as a rival I had only my brother,
I have true rights over him   30
and could save him from ill-founded laws.
A more legitimate obstacle arrests my boldness.
I yield to you, or rather I give to you the place
and the scepter which long ago your ancestors received
from the famous mortal conceived by the Earth;
the adoption put it into the hands of Aegeus.
Athens, enriched and protected by my father,
joyously recognized so noble a king,
and relegated your wretched brothers to oblivion.
Athens now recalls you to within its walls.   40
Long enough has it suffered from such a quarrel.
The blood of your family sinking into its furrows
has nourished the field from which it arose.
Troezen will obey me. The countryside of Crete
has offered a rich asylum to the son of Phèdre.
Attica belongs to you. I leave now, and for you I will assemble
all the votes divided among us.

ARICIA.   I am amazed and upset by all I hear.
I fear, yes, I fear a dream is deceiving me.
Am I awake? Can I trust such a plan?   50
What god conceived it in your heart, my lord?
How rightfully you are praised everywhere!
The truth about you is greater than your fame.
But for me, you sacrifice your own interests.
Isn't it enough that you don't hate me,

and that for so long a time you forbade your heart
a hatred . . . ?
HIPPOLYTUS.   Hatred for you, my lady?
Despite the bad traits ascribed to my pride,
do people think some monster bore me in its womb?   60
What savage character, what hardened hate
would not be softened in your presence?
Could I resist the deceptive charm . . .
ARICIA.   What are you saying, my lord?
HIPPOLYTUS.   I have gone too far.
Reason, it is easy to see, has given me to Love.
Since I have begun the breaking of my silence,
my lady, let me continue. Let me tell you
of a secret my heart can no longer contain.
You see before you a pitiful prince,   70
the memorable example of presumptuous pride.
In proud revolt against love,
I long insulted the chains of its captives.
As I deplored the shipwrecks of weak mortals,
I thought I would always watch these storms from the shore.
But now, enslaved to the common law,
I am carried off far from myself by some fury!
One moment conquered my bold imprudence.
My soul which has been so proud is now dependent.
For six months, ashamed and desperate,   80
bearing everywhere the arrow which pierces my flesh,
I have tested myself in vain against you and against myself.
When you are here, I leave; when you are absent, I see you.
Your image follows me in the depths of the forest.
The light of day and the shadows of night
retrace before me your charms which I avoid.
The rebel Hippolytus has been caught by you.
As a result of my useless efforts,
I search for myself and cannot find myself.
I cannot remember the lessons of Neptune.   90
The woods resound only with my laments,
and my idle horses have forgotten my voice.
Perhaps the story of so wild a love
makes you, as you listen to it, blush at what you have caused.
These are mad words from a heart which bows before you,
and I am a strange captive for so beautiful a bond.
But the offering should be dearer to your eyes.
Remember that I am speaking in a foreign language

and do not reject these ill-expressed vows
which, without you, Hippolytus would never have said.   100

Scene 3. *Hippolytus, Aricia, Theramenes, Ismene.*

THERAMENES. My lord, the Queen is here. She follows me.
  She wishes to see you.
HIPPOLYTUS.   To see me?
THERAMENES.   I do not know her purpose.
  But she has asked to see you.
  Phèdre wishes to speak to you before you leave.
HIPPOLYTUS. Phèdre? What can I say to her? What can she
    want?
ARICIA. My lord, you cannot refuse to see her.
  Even if you are convinced she is your enemy,
  you owe some degree of pity to her tears.   10
HIPPOLYTUS. In the meantime you are leaving, and I don't know
  whether I have offended you,
  whether the heart I have placed in your hands . . .
ARICIA. You may depart, Prince, and carry out your noble plans.
  Make Athens tributary of my power.
  I accept the gifts you offer me.
  But, to me, the large glorious empire
  is not the most precious of all your gifts.

Scene 4. *Hippolytus, Theramenes.*

HIPPOLYTUS. Is all in readiness? The Queen is coming.
  Leave and see that everything is swiftly prepared for the
    departure.
  Give the signal and the orders, and then come back
  to relieve me from this conversation I dread.

Scene 5. *Phèdre, Hippolytus, Oenone.*

PHÈDRE [*to* OENONE]. There he is. All my blood mounts to my
    heart.
  When I see him, I forget what I must say.
OENONE. Remember your son. You are his only hope.
PHÈDRE. I am told that you are about to leave us,
  my lord. I am here to join my tears with yours.
  I have come to you to speak of my alarm over my son.
  He has no father now, and the day is not far off

which will make him the witness of my own death.
A thousand enemies are already attacking him in his
    childhood.
You alone can take up his defense against them.   10
But a secret remorse upsets my mind.
I fear I have closed your ears to his cries.
I tremble lest your just anger
will persecute him because of his hated mother.

HIPPOLYTUS.   I would not stoop so low, my lady.

PHÈDRE.   I would not complain if you hated me.
You have seen me bent upon bringing you harm.
But you were not able to read the deep meaning of my heart.
I took care to show you only my enmity.
Wherever I lived in this land, I could not bear your presence.   20
I had spoken against you publicly and secretly,
and wanted to be separated from you by oceans.
By specific law I even forbade
your name being said in my presence.
Yet if suffering is measured by the offense,
if hate alone can call up hate in you,
never was a woman more worthy of pity,
and less worthy, my lord, of your enmity.

HIPPOLYTUS.   A mother, jealous of the rights of her own
    children,
rarely pardons the ways of a stepson.   30
I know this, my lady. Constant suspicions
are the commonest results of a second marriage.
Another woman would have been equally jealous of me
and I would have been perhaps more outraged by her.

PHÈDRE.   I swear to you, my lord, that Heaven
exempted me from this common law
and that a very different matter rages within me.

HIPPOLYTUS.   There is no reason to be upset any longer.
It is possible that your husband still lives.
Heaven may yet grant to our tears his return.   40
Neptune may protect him. My father's prayers
to his patron god may be efficacious.

PHÈDRE.   It is not possible to cross the river of the dead twice.
If Theseus saw those dark banks,
no god can send him back to you.
The greedy Acheron will not release its prey.
But what am I saying? He is not dead since he breathes in you.
I believe I still see my husband standing before me.

I see him. I speak to him, and my heart . . . What madness,
my lord! In spite of myself, I am telling you of my passion.   50

HIPPOLYTUS.   I can see the marvelous power of your love.
  Dead as he is, you can still see Theseus,
  Your soul is still enflamed by his love.

PHÈDRE.   Yes, Prince, I suffer and burn for Theseus.
  I love, not the man seen by hell,
  the fickle worshiper of so many mistresses,
  who will dishonor the god of the dead;
  but the faithful man, proud, even a bit barbaric,
  seductive, young, enflaming all the hearts he passes,
  the man like our gods, or like you as I see you now.   60
  He had your bearing, your eyes, your speech,
  and the noble modesty which colors your countenance,
  when he crossed the waters to Crete.
  The daughters of Minos had reason to think of him.
  What were you doing then? Why, without Hippolytus,
  did he assemble the heroes of Greece?
  You were still too young, but why weren't you
  on the ships which brought him to our shore?
  The monster of Crete would have perished at your hand
  in spite of all the detours of his vast retreat.   70
  To unravel the uncertain complexity,
  my sister would have armed your hand with the fatal thread.
  No! For I would have preceded her in this plan.
  Love would have instantly inspired me with the right thought.
  Prince, it is I, Phèdre, who would have served you
  and taught you the detours of the labyrinth.
  For your beauty I would have undertaken every risk.
  A mere thread would not have asserted a woman's love for you.
  I am the companion you needed in your peril.
  I would have walked ahead of you.   80
  Phèdre going down into the labyrinth at your side,
  would have been lost or saved with you.

HIPPOLYTUS.   What are these words? Have you forgotten
  that Theseus is my father and your husband?

PHÈDRE.   What makes you think I have forgotten him?
  Is it possible I have lost all sense of honor?

HIPPOLYTUS.   Forgive me, my lady. I blush when I confess
  that I wrongfully accused an innocent speech.
  My shame will not allow me to stay here
  and I am leaving. . . .   90

PHÈDRE.   You have heard too much, cruel Hippolytus!

I have told enough for you to understand all.
So, know Phèdre and know all her fury!
I am in love. But do not think that in this love
I approve of myself and find myself innocent,
or that any cowardly complacence has fortified the poison
of the mad love which bewilders my reason.
I am the wretched victim of heavenly vengeance
and hate myself more than you detest me.
The gods are my witnesses; those gods who in my heart   100
kindled the fire fatal to all of my family.
Those are the gods who took a cruel pride
in depraving the heart of a weak woman.
You yourself can remember the past.
It was not enough to avoid you, cruel Hippolytus, I exiled you.
I tried to appear odious and inhuman.
In order better to resist you, I sought to provoke your hate.
What profit came from all these useless efforts?
Your hate grew as my love grew.
Your sorrow gave you more charm than ever.   110
In tears and passion I languished and lost strength.
You needed only your eyes to be convinced of this,
if for one moment your eyes would look at me.
What am I saying? This shameful confession which I have just
    spoken,
can you believe it is voluntary?
Trembling for a son I did not dare betray,
I came to beg you not to hate him.
Feeble projects of a heart too full with what it loves!
Alas! I would speak to you only about yourself.
Avenge yourself, punish me for this odious love.   120
Worthy son of a hero who begot you,
free the universe of a monster who irritates you!
The widow of Theseus dares to love Hippolytus!
Believe me, this monster should not escape you.
Here is my heart. This is where your dagger should strike.
Eager to expiate its offense,
it moves forward to encounter your weapon.
Strike me. If you think my heart unworthy of your thrusts,
if your hate refuses me so sweet a punishment,
if your hand would be spotted with too vile a blood,   130
lend me your sword since I haven't your arm.
Give it over.
OENONE.   What are you doing, my lady?

Someone is coming. We must avoid witnesses.
Come with me. Let us leave this shameful scene.

[*They leave.*]

Scene 6. *Hippolytus, Theramenes.*

THERAMENES.   Is it Phèdre who is leaving? or who is being taken
away?
Why, my lord, all these signs of lamentation?
You are without a sword, speechless, colorless.
HIPPOLYTUS.   Let us leave, Theramenes. My surprise is extreme.
I cannot look at myself without a feeling of horror.
Phèdre . . . No! Let this horrible secret
remain buried in deep oblivion.
THERAMENES.   The ship is ready, if you wish to leave.
But Athens, my lord, has already spoken.
Its leaders have taken the votes of all the tribes.   10
Your brother has won. Phèdre has the upper hand.
HIPPOLYTUS.   Phèdre?
THERAMENES.   A herald, entrusted with the wishes of Athens,
is coming to place the control of the state in her hands.
Her son is king, my lord.
HIPPOLYTUS.   Oh! you gods who know her,
is it her virtue you are rewarding?
THERAMENES.   Yet meanwhile a new rumor says the King is
alive.
It is believed that Theseus has been seen in Epirus.
But I who looked for him there, know better. . . .   20
HIPPOLYTUS.   No matter. We must listen carefully to every
rumor.
Let us track down the source of this last report.
If it does not warrant putting off my departure,
we will leave. Whatever the cost may be,
we will put the scepter into the hands worthiest of bearing it.

ACT III

Scene 1. *Phèdre, Oenone.*

PHÈDRE. Take away all the honors that are being sent to me.
Stop bothering me. I will see no one.
My poor mind will not be deceived, do you hear?
It is better to hide me. I have said too much.
My passionate outburst became too visible.
I said what never should have been heard.
And how he listened to me! With endless tricks
he eluded my speech like a man heartless.
All he wanted was to get away as fast as possible.
The blush on his face increased my shame.   10
Why did you obstruct my plan for death?
When his sword was about to pierce my heart,
did he turn pale because of me? did he snatch it away from me?
It was enough that my hand touched it but once—
it has become something loathsome for him.
The wretched sword would now profane his hands.

OENONE. In your affliction, these complaints
feed a passion you should extinguish.
Wouldn't it be better for you, a worthy descendant of Minos,
to seek repose in some other way,   20
to rule in opposition to an ingrate who plans to flee,
and fix your attention on the governing of the state?

PHÈDRE. You want me to rule? to submit a state to my law,
when my weak mind cannot rule itself?
when I have given up the control of my own senses?
when I can barely breathe under my shameful yoke?
when I am dying!

OENONE.   You must leave.
PHÈDRE.   I cannot leave him.

21

OENONE.   You dared banish him. Haven't you the courage to   30
   avoid him?

PHÈDRE.   There is no time left. He knows my insane passion.
   I have moved beyond the fixed limits of modesty.
   I have shown my shame to the eyes of my conqueror,
   and hope, in spite of myself, has entered my heart.
   You yourself, revived my weakened strength,
   and my life which was expiring through my lips;
   you gave me new hope by your deceptive advice
   and made me see that I could love him.

OENONE.   Innocent or guilty of your afflictions,
   I was capable of any act in order to rescue you.   40
   But if ever an offense distressed you,
   could you forget the scorn of a proud man?
   He looked at you with stubborn heartlessness
   and left you almost prostrate at his feet.
   His barbaric pride made him odious to me.
   I wish you had seen him through my eyes at that moment.

PHÈDRE.   Oenone, he may set aside this pride which is offensive
   to you.
   Brought up in the forest, he has its savagery.
   Hardened by those barbaric principles, Hippolytus
   is hearing about love for the first time.   50
   Perhaps astonishment explains his silence,
   and perhaps we have complained too bitterly.

OENONE.   Remember that a barbarian woman gave him birth.

PHÈDRE.   She was a Scythian and barbarian, but she knew love.

OENONE.   He was destined to hate all women.

PHÈDRE.   Then I shall never have a rival.
   Your advice is unseasonal, Oenone.
   Serve my madness and not my reason.
   To love he opposes an inaccessible heart;
   to attack it let us find the most vulnerable spot.   60
   The attractiveness of an empire seemed to affect him.
   Athens appealed to him and this he did not conceal.
   His ships were already pointed in that direction
   and the sails abandoned to the wind.
   Seek out this ambitious youth in my name,
   Oenone, and tempt him with my sparkling crown.
   Let him put on his own brow the sacred diadem.
   All I wish is the honor of attaching it.
   I will yield to him the power I cannot keep.
   He will teach my son the art of command.   70

Perhaps he will serve as a father to him.
In his control I place both mother and son.
Try every means to bend his will.
Your words will be more heeded than mine.
Urge him and weep in his presence.
Do not fear begging him with your voice.
I approve of whatever you do. You are my one hope.
Go now. When you return, I will decide my fate.

Scene 2. *Phèdre.*

PHÈDRE.　Relentless Venus, who knows the shame
of my ancestors, am I sufficiently humiliated?
You could not increase your cruelty.
Your triumph is complete; every arrow has reached its mark.
If you now seek a new glory,
turn to an enemy more rebellious than I.
Hippolytus avoids you, and defying your wrath
he has never knelt before your altars.
Your name seems to offend his proud ears.
Goddess, avenge yourself! My cause is yours!　　　　10
Make him fall in love.
Have you returned already,
Oenone? He hates me and will not listen to you.

Scene 3. *Phèdre, Oenone.*

OENONE.　You must stifle all thought of this impossible love,
my lady. Bring back your past virtue.
The King, who was believed dead, is about to appear before you.
Theseus has come. Theseus is in Troezen.
The crowds are rushing to see him.
By your order, I had gone out and was looking for Hippolytus,
when a great wave of shouting . . .
PHÈDRE.　My husband is alive, Oenone! Say no more.
I have confessed a guilty love which will outrage him.
He is alive. I wish to know nothing else.　　　　10
OENONE.　What are you saying?
PHÈDRE.　　　　　　　　　　I predicted this, but you would
　　not listen.
Your tears prevailed over my remorse.
This morning, had I died, I would have been wept for
　　honorably.

I took your advice and now I will die dishonored.
OENONE.   You will die?
PHÈDRE.   This is my fatal day.
   My husband is going to appear and his son with him.
   I will see the witness to my adulterous love
   watch the way I dare greet his father.   20
   My heart will be heavy with the sighs he did not hear,
   and my eyes wet with tears spurned by him.
   He is sensitive to Theseus' honor; do you think
   he will conceal the love with which I am burning?
   Will he allow the betrayal of his father and his king?
   Will he be able to suppress the horror he feels toward me?
   But what if he does keep silent? I know my infidelity,
   Oenone, and I am not one of those bold women
   who enjoy tranquillity in crime
   and who show a countenance that never blushes.   30
   I know all my madness and can call it back to mind.
   Even now I can feel that these walls and ceilings
   are going to speak out, and, prepared to accuse me,
   they are waiting for my husband in order to disillusion him.
   Let me die. Let me be freed from such horror.
   Is dying so great a disaster?
   Death creates no fear for the unhappy.
   All I fear is the name I will leave after me.
   What a dire heritage for my wretched children!
   The blood of Jupiter will have to swell their courage.   40
   Yet despite the pride in such noble blood,
   a mother's crime is a heavy burden.
   I tremble lest one day words of too much truth
   will reproach them for having had a guilty mother.
   Oppressed by such a weight, I tremble
   lest neither one nor the other ever dares to raise his eyes.
OENONE.   Have no doubt, my lady, I pity both of them.
   Never was fear more justified than yours.
   But why expose them to such insults?
   Why take up arms against yourself?   50
   The die is cast. It will be said that Phèdre, guilty,
   fled the presence of her deceived husband.
   Hippolytus is fortunate in that
   your death will lend support to his words.
   And how will I answer your accuser?
   In his presence I shall be easily silenced.
   I will see him rejoice over his frightful triumph,

relating your share to any ear that will listen.
Rather than see this I would be devoured by a flame from
    heaven!
Do not deceive me now. Do you still love him?   60
What are your sentiments now for this bold prince?

PHÈDRE.   He has become for me a terrible monster.

OENONE.   Why grant him then a complete victory?
You fear him. Be the first to accuse him
of the crime he may impute to you today.
Who will contradict you? Everything is against him:
his sword is fortunately left with you,
your present sorrow, your past irritation,
your persistent warnings to his father,
and his exile already obtained by you.   70

PHÈDRE.   Are you asking me to persecute and blacken an
    innocent man?

OENONE.   My zeal needs only your silence.
I tremble as you do, and feel some of your remorse—
I would be swifter in facing a hundred deaths—
but I will lose you except for this unfortunate remedy;
there is nothing I would not do to save you.
I will speak. Theseus, angered by what I will tell him,
will limit his vengeance to exiling his son.
A father, when he punishes, remains a father.
His anger will be appeased with some slight rebuke.   80
But even if innocent blood has to be shed,
your threatened honor has the right to demand anything.
It is too rich a treasure to be compromised.
Whatever law it dictates, you must submit to it.
Your honor is in peril and to save it
you must sacrifice everything, even virtue.
People are coming. I see Theseus.

PHÈDRE.   And I see Hippolytus.
In his insolent eyes I see my defeat.
Do what you wish. I yield to you.   90
In my anxiety I can do nothing myself.

Scene 4. *Theseus, Hippolytus, Phèdre, Oenone, Theramenes.*

THESEUS.   Fortune is no longer against me,
my lady, and into your arms it puts . . .

PHÈDRE.   Stop, Theseus,
and do not profane such pure joy.

I do not deserve your tender attentions.
You have been offended. Jealous fortune
has not spared your wife in your absence.
Unworthy of pleasing or embracing you,
I can now think only of hiding.

Scene 5. *Theseus, Hippolytus, Theramenes.*

THESEUS.   My son, what is this strange welcome
    I have received?
HIPPOLYTUS.   Phèdre alone can explain the mystery.
    But if my ardent prayers are able to move you,
    allow me, my lord, not to see her anymore.
    Allow your disturbed son forever
    to disappear from the city your wife inhabits.
THESEUS.   You intend to leave me?
HIPPOLYTUS.   I did not seek her out.
    It was you who brought her to these shores.   10
    You were pleased, my lord, when you left, to entrust
    Aricia and the Queen to my care.
    I was charged with the duty of watching over them.
    But now no duty keeps me here.
    My idle youth has practiced its skill
    for long enough in the forests on insignificant enemies.
    This is an unworthy leisure. Allow me to leave
    and dip my javelins in more glorious blood.
    You had not yet reached my present age,
    when more than one tyrant, more than one savage monster   20
    had felt the strength of your arm.
    You had already persecuted violence
    and made safe the banks of the two seas.
    The free traveler had no fear of attack.
    Hercules, hearing the skill of your exploits
    was resting from his labors because of you.
    And I, the unknown son of so famous a father,
    am still unequal to the fame of my mother.
    Let my courage at last be put to the test.
    If some monster has escaped you,   30
    allow me to place at your feet its honorable remains,
    or allow the enduring memory of a noble death,
    immortalizing a life so worthily cut short,
    to prove to the universe that I was your son.
THESEUS.   What is this? What horror in this house

causes everyone to flee from my presence?
If I am so little wanted and so feared,
why was I taken from my prison?
I had only one friend. His imprudent desire
was to abduct the wife of the tyrant of Epirus.   40
Against my will I served his passionate plan.
But angry fate blinded both of us.
The tyrant caught me unarmed and without defense.
I saw Pirithous, whom I wept for,
delivered by that barbarian to the cruel beasts
he fed on the blood of wretched men.
He locked me up in dark caverns,
deep in the earth and close to the empire of the dead.
At last, after six months, the gods took pity on me.
I was able to trick my guards   50
and I purged the world of a perfidious enemy.
He himself became food for his beasts.
And now when joyfully I draw near
to those I hold dearest in the world,
what do I find? When my soul, recovering,
wants to behold again these dear ones,
they welcome me in trembling and fear.
Everyone leaves, all refuse to embrace me.
As I feel the terror I inspire,
I wish I were still in the prisons of Epirus.   60
You must speak. Phèdre complains that I have been outraged.
Who has betrayed me? Why have I not been avenged?
Has Greece, which I have served so often,
given refuge to the criminal?
You don't answer? Is my own son
an accomplice of my enemies?
I must know. This doubt is too heavy to bear.
What is the crime and who is guilty?
Phèdre will have to explain why she is troubled.

Scene 6. *Hippolytus, Theramenes.*

HIPPOLYTUS.   What was the meaning of Phèdre's speech?
     It chilled me. She is still a prey to her extreme fury.
     Does she intend to accuse herself and destroy herself?
     What will the King say? What deadly poison
     has love spread throughout the house!
     I am consumed by a love he will hate and blame.

Today I am the same as he once knew me,
though I am terrified by black forebodings.
But innocence has nothing to fear.
Let me find some way   10
by which I may move my father to pity
and tell him of my love, which he may oppose
but which he is powerless to destroy.

ACT IV

Scene 1. *Theseus, Oenone.*

THESEUS.   Ah! What are you telling me? What kind of traitor
  prepared this outrage to his father's honor?
  How relentless this fate of mine!
  I don't know where I am or where I am going.
  Is this the reward for a father's care?
  Could any plan or thought be more loathsome?
  In order to succeed with this criminal love,
  he resorted to force.
  I know this sword which he used in his passion.
  I armed him with it, but for a nobler use.   10
  Couldn't he be restrained by the bonds of family?
  Why did Phèdre put off his punishment?
  Why did she protect him by her silence?
OENONE.   My lord, she was protecting you, his father.
  Ashamed of the attempt of her passionate lover,
  ashamed of the criminal light in his eyes,
  Phèdre was dying. With her own hands
  she would have taken her life.
  I saw her raise her arm and I ran to save her.
  I saved her life for your love.   20
  And because I pitied both her dismay and your alarm,
  I have interpreted, in spite of myself, her tears to you.
THESEUS.   The liar! He couldn't help turning pale,
  through fear, when he saw me. I saw him tremble.
  I was surprised by his lack of joy.
  He embraced me coldly and my love was chilled.
  But had he felt already in Athens
  this guilty love which devours him?

29

OENONE.   My lord, remember how the Queen complained.
 This criminal love was the cause of her hate.   30
THESEUS.   And so the passion began again in Troezen?
OENONE.   I have told you everything that took place.
 But I have left the Queen too long with her grief.
 Allow me to leave you and go to her.

Scene 2. *Theseus, Hippolytus.*

THESEUS.   There he is! By his noble bearing
 anyone else would be deceived as I was.
 How is it that on the countenance of an adulterer
 there shines the expression of virtue and innocence?
 Shouldn't we be able to recognize
 by certain signs the heart of a traitor?
HIPPOLYTUS.   May I ask you what chagrin,
 my lord, has changed your noble face?
 Won't you trust me with your secret?
THESEUS.   Liar! How do you dare come into my presence? 10
 Monster, whom Heaven has spared too long!
 You are the last of the bandits. I have slain all the others.
 After the passion of a horrible love
 bore you to your father's bed,
 you dare come before the man you wronged,
 you come into this place reeking with your infamy.
 You will not find, under a foreign sky,
 any land where my name is unknown.
 Leave now. Do not come here defying my hate
 and tempting an anger which I can scarcely restrain. 20
 I have my share of eternal opprobrium
 for having begotten so criminal a son,
 and must not allow your death, which would shame my
  memory,
 to desecrate the glory of my work.
 Go, I say. If you do not want a sudden punishment
 to add you to the rogues I have punished,
 see to it that the sun which lightens our world
 never beholds you again walking on these shores.
 Once more, go! Go forever
 and purge my land of your presence.   30
 Hear me, Neptune. If once my courage
 rid your banks of infamous cutthroats,
 remember that as a reward for my efforts,

you promised to grant the first of my prayers.
During the long cruel days in prison
I did not call upon your immortal power.
Greedy for the help I expect from you,
I held back my prayers for a greater need.
Today I beseech you. Avenge a wretched father.
I give over this traitor to the fullness of your anger.   40
Stifle with his own blood his licentious desires.
Theseus will measure your generosity by your wrath.

HIPPOLYTUS.   So Phèdre accuses Hippolytus of a criminal love!
  Such horror makes me speechless.
  So many attacks rain on me at once
  that I have no words to say and no voice with which to speak
   them. . . .

THESEUS.   Traitor, you imagined that in cowardly silence
  Phèdre would bury your brutish insolence.
  When you fled, you should not have left
  in her hands the sword which condemns you.   50
  Or rather you should have completed your attack,
  and taken from her both speech and life.

HIPPOLYTUS.   I should tell the truth
  of so black a lie that has overwrought you.
  But I will not reveal a secret concerning you.
  Please approve of the respect which forbids me to speak.
  Do not increase the torments you already have.
  Examine my life and remember who I am.
  Small crimes always precede major crimes.
  A man who has first transgressed the laws,   60
  can violate then the most sacred rights.
  Crime has its degrees as virtue has.
  Never have you seen timid innocence
  suddenly pass to extreme licence.
  One day is not enough to make of a virtuous man
  a perfidious murderer and an incestuous coward.
  Conceived in the womb of a chaste heroine,
  I have not betrayed the origin of her blood.
  Pittheus, looked upon by all men as a sage,
  was my teacher when I left my mother's care.   70
  I do not wish to boast or speak of myself,
  but I think I have shown hatred
  for the crimes that are ascribed to me.
  Hippolytus is known for this in all of Greece.
  I have made virtue blunt.

The unbending rigor of my temperament is known.
Daylight is not purer than the depths of my heart.
And yet you say Hippolytus, intoxicated with profane love,
has . . .

THESEUS.   This is the very pride which condemns you.
I can see the odious principle of your coldness.   80
Phèdre alone bewitched your senses,
and for any other woman your heart
scorned an innocent love.

HIPPOLYTUS.   No, father—I have concealed this too long—my
heart
did not scorn an innocent love.
At your feet I will confess my real crime.
I am in love, but in defiance of your law.
Aricia has enslaved me to her law.
The daughter of Pallas has conquered your son.
I worship her. Rebellious to your command,   90
my heart breathes and yearns only for her.

THESEUS.   You love Aricia? This is an obvious trick.
You acknowledge one crime in order to escape another.

HIPPOLYTUS.   My lord, I have avoided her for six months, and I
still love her.
I came here in great fear to tell you.
Will nothing clear away your error?
What awesome oath is needed to reassure you?
By heaven and earth and all of nature . . .

THESEUS.   Perjury is always the recourse of scoundrels.
Spare me any more of your words,   100
if they are the only pledge of your false virtue.

HIPPOLYTUS.   It seems false and deceptive to you.
Phèdre in her heart does me better justice.

THESEUS.   Your impudence arouses my anger.

HIPPOLYTUS.   How long will you banish me and to what place?

THESEUS.   If you were beyond the column of Alcides,
I would still think you too close.

HIPPOLYTUS.   Charged with the terrible crime you suspect me
of,
who will pity me when you send me away?

THESEUS.   Seek out those friends whose fatal character   110
honors adultery and applauds incest,
traitors and ingrates without honor, without principle,
worthy of protecting a man like you.

HIPPOLYTUS.   You keep speaking to me of incest and adultery.

I will hold my tongue. But Phèdre comes from a mother,
Phèdre is from a lineage—and my lord, you know this—
more filled with horrors than mine.
THESEUS.   Now your rage has lost all restraint.
For the last time, leave my presence.
Leave now. Do not wait for an angry father   120
to expel you shamelessly from this land.

Scene 3. *Theseus.*

THESEUS.   Hippolytus, you are rushing to your death.
Neptune, god of the sea, who is feared by other gods,
gave me his word and will carry it out.
An avenging god is at your heels. You will not escape him.
I loved you once, and in spite of your crime
my heart feels for you now.
But you forced me to condemn you.
Never has a father been more outraged.
Gods in heaven, see my grief!
Why did I ever beget so criminal a child?   10

Scene 4. *Phèdre, Theseus.*

PHÈDRE.   My lord, I have come to you in terror and fear.
Your loud voice reached my ears.
I am afraid your threat was carried out too swiftly.
If there is still time, spare your son.
Don't turn against your family, I beg you.
Save me from the horror of hearing your blood cry out.
Do not plunge me into everlasting grief
for spilling your own son's blood.
THESEUS.   Phèdre, I have spilled no blood.
Yet the ingrate has not escaped.   10
An immortal has charge of his death.
Neptune has promised me this. You will be avenged.
PHÈDRE.   Neptune has promised? What angry prayers . . . ?
THESEUS.   Are you afraid they will not be heeded?
Join yours with my just prayers.
Tell me his crimes in all their blackness.
Stir up my anger which has been too slow.
You do not yet know all of his crimes.
His fury lashed out at you,
and said your mouth is full of lies and deceit.   20

He insists that Aricia is the mistress of his heart,
and that he loves her.

PHÈDRE.   What, my lord?

THESEUS.   He said it to me.

But I saw through this obvious trick.
Let us hope for swift justice from Neptune.
I myself am going to his altars
to urge him to carry out his immortal promises.

Scene 5. *Phèdre, Oenone.*

PHÈDRE.   What is this he said to me?
What fire flares up again in my heart?
What thunderbolt, O gods, what fatal news!
I came here to save my son.
I pulled myself away from terrified Oenone
and gave over to the remorse which has tormented me.
How far would this repentance have taken me?
I would have perhaps at last accused myself.
Perhaps, if my voice had not been cut off,
the terrible truth would have escaped from me.   10
Hippolytus feels nothing for me!
Aricia has his love and his faith!
When before my prayers the ruthless ingrate
armed himself with a haughty look and a proud countenance,
I believed that his heart, always closed to love,
was hostile equally to all women.
But one woman did affect his feelings.
One woman did find grace before his cruel eyes.
Perhaps he does have a heart easy to move.
I am the only one he could not bear.   20
Should I take on, then, the duty of defending him?

Scene 6. *Phèdre, Oenone.*

PHÈDRE.   Dear Oenone, do you know what I have just learned?

OENONE.   No, but I can't conceal that I am terrified for you.
I tremble at the reason which made you come here.
I fear some madness that will be fatal.

PHÈDRE.   Who would have believed it, Oenone? I had a rival.

OENONE.   What, my lady?

PHÈDRE.   Hippolytus is in love, and I cannot doubt it.
That wild enemy who could not be tamed,

who was offended by respect and irritated by complaints,
that tiger whom I never approached without fear,   10
submissive and docile has recognized a conqueror.
Aricia found the way to his heart.
OENONE.   Aricia?
PHÈDRE.   This suffering I had not yet felt!
   I had saved myself for this new torment.
   Whatever I suffered up until now: fears and passion,
   the fury of love and the horror of remorse,
   the unbearable pain of a cruel refusal—
   all that was but a weak foretaste of the torment I endure now.
   They are in love! By what spell were my eyes deceived?   20
   How did they meet? How long have they loved? Where did
      they meet?
   You knew this. Why did you let me be tricked?
   Couldn't you have told me about their furtive passion?
   Were they often seen speaking and looking for one another?
   Did they hide in the depths of the forest?
   Ah! It was permissible for them to see one another.
   Heaven approved the innocence of their sighs.
   Without remorse they could heed their instincts for love.
   Every day rose clear and serene for them.
   But I hid from the day and escaped from the light   30
   as if I were rejected by all nature.
   The only god I dared beseech was death.
   I waited for the moment of death,
   and fed on sorrow and tears.
   Yet when I was too closely watched in my suffering
   I did not dare give full vent to your tears.
   As I trembled, I felt that fatal pleasure,
   and with a serene face disguising my anguish,
   I had often to deprive myself of my own tears.
OENONE.   But what will come of their vain love?   40
   They will not meet again.
PHÈDRE.   Their love will continue always.
   At this very moment—oh! let me not think of it!—
   they are defying the fury of a jealous woman.
   Even despite the exile which will separate them,
   they swear a thousand times not to leave one another.
   I cannot bear their happiness which insults me,
   Oenone. Take pity on my jealous rage.
   Aricia must be killed. We must arouse the anger
   of my husband against a hated family.   50

He must not stop with easy penalties.
The sister's crime exceeds her brothers'.
I will implore him in my jealous rage.
What am I doing? Have I lost control of my mind?
I am jealous! and Theseus is the man I am to implore!
My husband is living, and I still burn with passion.
And for whom? to whose heart are my prayers addressed?
Every word I say adds to my panic.
My crimes have become monstrous.
They include incest and imposture.   60
My hands of an assassin, so eager for revenge,
are about to plunge into innocent blood.
And I continue to live. I am still seen
by the holy sun from which I am descended.
My ancestor is the father and the master of the gods.
The heavens, the entire universe is full of my ancestors.
Where can I hide? Let me turn to the darkness of Hades.
What am I saying? There my father holds the fatal urn.
The gods placed it in his severe hands.
In hell Minos judges the pale ghosts of men.   70
How his terrified spirit will tremble
when his daughter comes before him
and confesses these misdemeanors
and crimes which are unknown to hell!
Father, what will you say at such a horrible spectacle?
I can see the solemn urn drop from your hands.
I can see you looking for some new punishment
and becoming the executioner of your own family.
Forgive me. A cruel god laid waste to your family.
Behold his vengeance in the madness of your child.   80
Alas! my unhappy heart did not gather the fruit
of the terrible crime whose shame haunts me.
Pursued by woe until my last breath,
I relinquish in torment a painful life.

OENONE.   My lady, you must repulse this ill-founded terror.
Consider differently an excusable error.
You are in love. Such a fate cannot be overcome.
You were impelled by some magical power of the gods.
Is this so unusual a prodigy for mankind?
Are you the only victim of love?   90
Weakness is innate in all of us.
You are mortal and you are involved in the fate of mortals.
You complain of a yoke imposed for all time.

Even the gods, inhabitants of Olympus,
who by scandal terrify criminals,
have sometimes suffered from illicit passion.

PHÈDRE.   What are you saying? What advice do you dare offer
   me?
Are you bent on poisoning me to the very end,
wretched Oenone? This is how you ruined me.
You turned me back to the daylight I was fleeing.   100
Your entreaties made me forget my duty.
I was avoiding Hippolytus, and you forced me to look upon
   him.
What right did you have? Why did your imperious words,
as they accused him, blacken his life?
He may die because of this, and the sacrilegious vow
of a wrathful father is perhaps already carried out.
I will heed you no longer, for you are a monster.
Leave my presence.
I wish now to be alone with my tortured fate.
May the justice of heaven reward you,   110
and may your punishment forever terrify
all those who, like you, with loathsome means,
feed the weakness of unhappy rulers,
urge them to submit to the desires of their heart,
and dare open up the way to crime!
Detestable flatterers, they are the most pernicious gift
the anger of the gods can give to princes!

OENONE [alone].   I gave up everything and did everything in
   order to serve her.
I deserve the reward she has now given me.

ACT V

Scene 1. *Hippolytus, Aricia.*

ARICIA. Can you be silent in such extreme danger?
  Can you permit your loving father to remain in error?
  Cruel Hippolytus, if you scorn the power of my tears,
  if, without pain, you consent to seeing me no more,
  you will leave and we shall separate,
  but at least safeguard your life.
  Defend your honor from a shameful reproach,
  and force your father to withdraw his vows.
  There is still time. Why, through what caprice,
  are you leaving the way open to your accuser?   10
  Inform Theseus.
HIPPOLYTUS. I have said everything I could.
  Should I have revealed the wrong of his wife?
  In telling him the full details,
  should I have covered his face with unworthy shame?
  You alone saw through the hateful mystery.
  I have only you and the gods with whom I can speak.
  This is the measure of my love: I could not hide from you
  what I wanted to hide from myself.
  But remember the seal of secrecy under which I told you all.   20
  You must forget, if you can, that I spoke to you.
  Your lips that are so pure,
  must never tell this horrible adventure.
  I will trust the justice of the gods.
  It is for their own good to justify me.
  Phèdre one day will be punished for her crime,
  and will not escape a deserving ignominy.
  This is the one mark of respect I demand from you.
  Everything else I permit my free anger.

39

Leave the slavery to which you have been reduced.   30
Dare to follow me, dare to come with me in my flight.
You must pull yourself away from this fatal, profaned place
where virtue breathes a poisoned air.
To conceal your abrupt departure,
profit from the confusion created by my disgrace.
I can assure you of the means for this flight.
Your only guards here are my men.
Powerful defenders will take our side.
Argos has asked us to come, and Sparta.
We will speak of our cause to our common friends   40
and prevent Phèdre, as she gathers what fortune we abandon,
from expelling both of us from the paternal throne
and promising her son my death and yours.
This is the right moment for us to seize.
What fear holds you back? You seem uncertain.
Your rights and your interest guide me in this plan.
I am burning with anticipation, and you seem coldly
    indifferent.
Are you afraid of following in the steps of an exile?

ARICIA.   How precious, my lord, such an exile would be!
If I could join with your fate, how joyously   50
I would live far from the rest of mankind!
But we are not united in marriage.
Can I honorably escape this place with you?
I know that I can free myself
from your father without harming even the strictest honor.
It would not be an escape from my own family.
Escape is permitted if it is escape from a tyrant.
But you love me, my lord, and my honor . . .

HIPPOLYTUS.   No, no! I have not forgotten your reputation.
A nobler plan brings me here before you.   60
Flee from your enemies and follow your husband.
Since it is the will of Heaven, we are free in our woes.
The pledge of our word depends on no one.
Marriage is not always surrounded by torches.
At the gates of Troezen, in the midst of tombs,
ancient sepulchers of the princes of my race,
is a sacred temple which does not allow perjury.
In that place men do not dare take false oaths.
The dishonest man would receive a swift punishment.
He would fear inevitable death.   70
The consequence of a lie would be too fearful.

There, if you believe my words, we will take
the solemn oath of eternal love.
Our witness will be the god we revere in that temple.
We will pray that he be a father for us.
I will call upon the names of the most sacred of the gods.
Chaste Diana, proud Juno,
all of the gods, witnesses of my affection,
will vouch for the sincerity of my holy promises.

ARICIA.   The King is coming. You must leave, Hippolytus, at this   80
     very moment.
I will stay briefly to conceal my departure.
Go. Leave me a faithful guide
who will direct my timid steps to you.

Scene 2. *Theseus, Aricia, Ismene.*

THESEUS.   O gods, bring me light and show me
the truth I am searching for in this palace.

ARICIA.   Make preparations, dear Ismene, and be ready for our
     flight.

Scene 3. *Theseus, Aricia.*

THESEUS.   You change color, my lady, and seem embarrassed.
What was Hippolytus doing here?

ARICIA.   My lord, he was saying a last farewell.

THESEUS.   Your eyes subjugated his rebellious heart.
His first sighs were because of you.

ARICIA.   My lord, I cannot hide the truth from you.
He did not inherit the unjust hate you feel.
He did not treat me as a criminal.

THESEUS.   I know. He swore eternal love to you.
Do not put your trust in his inconstant heart.   10
He swore the same love to others that he swore to you.

ARICIA.   Hippolytus, my lord?

THESEUS.   You should have made him less fickle.
How could you stand sharing him with someone else?

ARICIA.   And how can you allow such horrible words
to darken the days of so noble a life?
Have you so little knowledge of his heart?
Can't you discern the difference between crime and
     innocence?
Must you be the only one who cannot see

his virtue which shines forth for everyone else? 20
You have given him over to the malice of gossip.
You must repent of your homicidal prayers.
You should fear, my lord, that Heaven in its rigor
hates you enough to carry out your wishes.
In its wrath Heaven often receives our victims.
Its gifts are often the punishment for our crimes.

THESEUS. It will do you no good to cover up his sin.
Your love blinds you in favor of the ingrate.
I have put my faith in certain irreproachable witnesses.
I have seen the sincere tears of a woman. 30

ARICIA. Take care, my lord. Your invincible hands
have delivered mankind from countless monsters.
But all of them are not destroyed, and you allow
one of them to . . . Your son, my lord, has forbidden me to
    speak.
I know of the respect he will always have for you.
If I spoke now, I would grieve him.
Let me imitate his discreetness and leave your presence
so that I will not be forced to break my silence.

Scene 4. *Theseus.*

THESEUS. What is she trying to say? What is concealed
in the words which she only half uttered?
Are they bent on confusing me by some vain pretense?
Are they both agreed to torture me?
In spite of the severity of my judgment,
I can hear a plaintive cry in the depths of my heart.
A secret pity has taken hold of me and is affecting me.
I will question Oenone a second time.
I must learn more about the entire crime.
Guards, have Oenone come here alone. 10

Scene 5. *Theseus, Panope.*

PANOPE. My lord, I do not know what the Queen is planning,
but from her terrible state I fear the worst.
Her face shows a deathlike despair.
Already she has the pallor of death.
Oenone, whom she sent away in shame,
has already hurled herself into the sea.
We do not know how this madness came about,

but the waves have taken her from us forever.
THESEUS.   What are you saying?
PANOPE.   Her death did not quiet the Queen.   10
The anguish of her heart seemed to get worse.
From time to time, to diminish her secret grief,
she lifts up her children and covers them with tears,
and then suddenly, forgetting her maternal love,
she pushes them aside with horror.
She wanders about aimlessly.
Bewildered, she does not recognize us.
Three times she began to write, and changing her mind,
three times she tore up the letter.
I beg you to see her, my lord, I beg you to help her.   20
THESEUS.   So, Oenone is dead, and Phèdre wants to die.
Call back my son, let him come and defend himself!
I want him to speak. I am ready now to hear him.
Do not pour down your fatal blessings,
Neptune! I prefer now not to have my prayers heeded.
I have perhaps believed witnesses who were not trustworthy.
I raised my cruel hands to you too early.
Such vows I have taken would lead me to despair!

Scene 6. *Theseus, Theramenes.*

THESEUS.   Is it you, Theramenes? What have you done with my
    son?
I gave him to you at an early age.
But what is the reason for your sadness and your tears?
What has happened to my son?
THERAMENES.   Your solicitude comes too late.
Your affection is useless. Hippolytus is dead.
THESEUS.   Ah!
THERAMENES.   I have seen the most loving of mortals perish,
and I can say also, my lord, the least guilty.
THESEUS.   My son is dead? When I am opening my arms to re-   10
    ceive him,
did the impatient gods hasten his end?
How has he been taken from me? What thunderbolt fell?
THERAMENES.   We had just left the gates of Troezen.
He was on his chariot. His grieving guards,
drawn up around him, were silent as he was.
Sadly he was taking the road to Mycenae.
His hand had loosened the reins on his horses.

These proud beasts which could be seen once
ardent and noble obeying his voice,
now with sad eyes and lowered heads,   20
seemed to respond to his grieving thought.
A terrible cry, coming from below the waves,
at that moment cut through the quiet of the scene.
From the bowels of the earth a formidable voice
wailed in answer to the fearful cry.
Our blood froze in our hearts.
The attentive horses reared in terror
while over the flat surface of the sea
a gigantic wave of foam rose up.
It came close, broke and spewed out in full sight,   30
in its waves of foam, a raging monster.
Its broad head was armed with dangerous horns.
Yellowish scales covered its body.
Was it an untamed bull or a bold dragon?
Its back was twisted in coils.
Its long shrieks shook the seacoast.
Heaven was horrified at seeing such a wild monster.
The earth was shocked and the air grew infected.
The wave, which had brought it, recoiled in terror.
Everyone fled—a man's courage would have been useless—   40
and sought shelter in the neighboring temple.
Only Hippolytus, as the worthy son of a hero,
stopped his horses, seized his spear,
and rushing at the monster, hurled his weapon with good aim
and tore a wide gash in the animal's side.
It leaped, and roaring with rage and pain,
fell at the feet of the horses,
rolled over, and opened a flaming mouth.
Fire, blood, and fumes covered them.
Fright overcame them, and this time deaf,   50
they heeded neither the reins nor their master's voice.
Vainly Hippolytus tried to control them.
They reddened their bridles with bloody foam.
Some say that in this great melee a god was seen
flogging their dust-covered sides.
Through fear they plunged from the rocks.
The axle creaked and broke. Courageous Hippolytus
saw his broken chariot split into fragments.
He himself fell, twisted into the harness.
Forgive my grief. This cruel picture   60

will be for me an eternal source of sorrow.
My lord, I saw your poor son
dragged by the horses his hand had fed.
He tried to call them, but his voice frightened them.
They kept running until all of his body was an open wound.
The field resounded with our cries of grief.
They finally slowed their wild race,
and stopped, not far from those ancient tombs
where lie the cold remains of his royal ancestors.
Anguished I rushed up and his guard followed me.   70
The trail of his noble blood led us.
The rocks were covered with it and the thorns
bore blood-stained bits of his hair.
I reached him and called to him. Then stretching out his
    hand,
he opened his eyes and closed them again.
"Heaven," he said, "is snatching from me an innocent life.
After my death, take care of poor Aricia.
Dear friend, if one day my father learns the truth,
and pities the fate of a falsely accused son,
tell him, if he wishes to appease my blood and my unquiet   80
    shade,
to treat his captive with gentleness,
to give back to her . . ." At those words the hero died
and left in my arms a disfigured body,
in which the anger of the gods triumphed,
and which his own father would not recognize.
THESEUS.   Oh son! You were the hope I have lost!
    Oh! relentless gods, you served me too well.
    Nothing remains now but mortal grief.
THERAMENES.   Modest Aricia came then.
    My lord, she was fleeing your wrath   90
    and accepting him as husband in the sight of the gods.
    On drawing near, she saw the grass streaked with blood,
    and then she saw (what an object for the eyes of a lover!)
    Hippolytus stretched out, mangled and without color.
    For some time she would not believe her affliction,
    and not recognizing the hero she loved,
    she kept calling for Hippolytus.
    Finally she realized he was there before her,
    and turning her face toward heaven,
    cold, grieving, and almost lifeless,   100
    she fell in a faint at the feet of her lover.

Ismene was close by. Ismene weeping
brought her back to life, or rather to tears.
And I, cursing my life,
came here to tell you the last wish of a hero,
and acquit myself of the painful duty
he asked of me as he died.
But I see his mortal enemy coming.

Scene 7. *Theseus, Phèdre, Theramenes, Panope, Guards.*

THESEUS.   My son is dead, Phèdre, and you are triumphant.
I was right in my fears and suspicions
when I excused him in my heart.
But now he is dead. Take your victim.
Gloat over his loss, whether just or unjust.
I will not be undeceived, Phèdre.
I believe him guilty since you have accused him.
His death gives me enough reason for lament
without my looking for some terrible enlightenment,
which would not bring him back to life   10
but would only increase my sorrow.
Far from you and far from these shores,
let me flee the image of my bleeding son.
Obsessed with this memory of death,
I will banish myself from the entire universe.
Everything rises up against my injustice.
The glory of my name increases my suffering.
If I were less well known by men, I could hide more easily.
I detest now the help which the gods have given me.
I am going away in order to bewail their murderous favors,   20
and I shall stop beseeching them with useless prayers.
Whatever their power be, their fatal generosity
cannot replace what they have taken from me.
PHÈDRE.   No, Theseus, I must break my silence.
I must give your son his innocence.
He was not guilty.
THESEUS.   Wretched father that I am!
It was on your word I condemned him.
Cruel Phèdre, how can you be forgiven?
PHÈDRE.   I have but few moments left. You must hear me,   30
    Theseus.
I was the impure, the incestuous one
who hated to look at chaste respectful Hippolytus.

Heaven put this fatal love in my heart.
Wicked Oenone did all the rest.
She feared that Hippolytus, learning of my madness,
would tell of a passion which so horrified him.
Profiting from my extreme weakness,
she hastened to denounce him to you.
She has punished herself, and escaping from my wrath,
she sought in the sea an easy death.   40
The sword would have already severed my life,
if I had not allowed my suspected virtue to lament.
I wanted to tell you of my remorse
and descend by a slower path to the dead.
I have taken a poison which Medea brought to Athens.
It is coursing now through my veins.
It has already reached my heart
and has cast an unknown cold upon it.
There is a cloud over my eyes.
I can hardly see the sky and you whom my presence insults.   50
Death, stealing the light from my eyes
gives back to the day all of its purity.
PANOPE.   She is dying, my lord!
THESEUS.   Would that the memory
of so black a deed might die with her!
Now that I know my error,
I want to mingle my tears with the blood of my son.
I want to embrace what is left of his body
and expiate the madness of a vow I loathe.
I will give him the honors he deserves,   60
and to appease his troubled spirit,
I will, despite the plottings of her guilty family,
ask Aricia to be my daughter from today on.

Index of Proper Names

Neptune, god of the sea.

Olympus, mountain in Thessaly, abode of the Olympian gods.

Pallantides, the sons of Pallas, brothers of Aricia. Theseus had them
killed because he believed them a threat to his rule of Athens.

Pallas, father of Aricia, king of Athens.

Pasiphaë, mother of Phèdre.

Periboea, maiden who was to be sacrificed to the Minotaur and whom
Theseus saved.

Pirithous, friend of Theseus.

Pittheus, maternal ancestor of Theseus.

Procrustus, brigand of Attica.

Salamis, city of Cyprus.

Scythia, ancient name of parts of Europe.

Sinnis, brigand of Corinth.

Sirron, brigand of Megarus.

Sparta, chief city of the Peloponnesus.

Taenarus, today Cape Matapan.

Venus, goddess of love.